# A Litany of SHE Poems

*poems by*

# Davida Kilgore

*Finishing Line Press*
Georgetown, Kentucky

# A Litany of SHE Poems

*For Corvale and Amari'Ana*

*For my granddaughter, Amari'Ana, who is already a force of nature to be reckoned with.*

*For my grandson, Corvale, who is already the wind.*

Copyright © 2024 by Davida Kilgore
ISBN 979-8-88838-704-7  First Edition
All rights reserved under International and Pan-American Copyright Conventions.
No part of this book may be reproduced in any manner whatsoever without written
permission from the publisher, except in the case of brief quotations embodied in
critical articles and reviews.

## ACKNOWLEDGMENTS

With much gratitude to Carolyn Holbrook who invited me to join the
TCBWW and for the beautiful Black women who read through the first draft
of a few of these poems.

And with much love to Diego Vazquez who invited me to join the WRITES
and blessings to Loren, Howard, Kevin, Paula, Rebecca, Andrea, Miriam-
Rachel, Jon, and Rich who listen(ed) to me read, Sunday after Sunday, and
offer(ed) critiques that were both helpful and meaningful, even when they
cut to the quick.

Publisher: Leah Huete de Maines
Editor: Christen Kincaid
Cover Art: *Eve's Lament* by Karen Gormandy
Author Photo: Virginia Townsend
Cover Design: Elizabeth Maines McCleavy

Order online: www.finishinglinepress.com
also available on amazon.com

Author inquiries and mail orders:
Finishing Line Press
PO Box 1626
Georgetown, Kentucky 40324
USA

# Contents

## A Litany of SHE Poems

SHEILA
Sheila won't look in the mirror mirror
On the wall, who's the ugliest of us
All. "Why you, of course." Her beauty
Is such that it pained the glass to stare
Back at her almond eyes, her thick lashes,
Her wide nose, her rosebud lips etched
In her cocoa skin. If only, Sheila thinks,
I wasn't in this wheelchair, my legs useless,
Frozen beneath me hidden by a white
Waffle-weave blanket.

Sheila & Jimmy the Cricket can't spontaneously
Go for an evening out among the planets.
They have to verify the MoonBeam
Is accessible both at the front door and in
The bathroom. This narrows the orbits
They can ride and Sheila senses Jimmy
Is growing weary of accommodating her
Need for intimacy, for having his fingers,
His tongue, his sex deep inside her. Her hips,
wide enough to birth triplet humanoids,
Her thighs crush alabaster & her breasts
Float in a clear azure sky. Jimmy loves her
In a fathomless way. He is small but broad
& can carry her anywhere she wants to go
Thru the stratosphere and beyond the heavens
They can fly away and live among the stars
Among the pinpricks of light that make up the galaxy
Where the indigenous live, work, and cater to
Humanoids like Sheila & Jimmy. On Mars
Sheila can walk, dance, run with her thoughts,
Legs are not necessary.

Jimmy's naked, he's ramrod straight pointing
At Sheila he says to her, "you're the one." He hovers
Above her head, his legs rubbing together, he grabs

Clumps of her hair and pulls her head up to his
She sucks his tongue until he trembles
Determined to fire his wad at the appropriate time,
At the appropriate configuration of asteroids.
Sheila & Jimmy fly off to Cassiopeia, make their
Own star assemblies that glow red, black, and green,
Freedom to love, freedom to love each other's
android bodies. Up there, somewhere beyond
The golden-rod skies, lies a place in the heavens.

SHE
SHE's the one who discovered Jimmy
Lying in a star cluster dangling
His legs over a blue star that struggled
To breathe beneath his weight.
He was fast asleep snoring loudly
Infuriating the ¾ moon, shining dully
Dropping from a height of four feet above
The earth rotating on its axis so that its inhabitants
Could watch the two lovers—SHE and Jimmy—
The one who discovered what was never
Lost just sleeping among red rayz &
The other up past twilight, up past moonlight,
Up past star light, star bright.

Jimmy sat on a cluster of lava rocks
And stared as SHE levitated above his star,
They stared at each other for ½ of eternity
Reading each other's thoughts. SHE bristled
At his thought of laying Sheila naked
On the constellation, her supple body lifeless
Legs still beneath his touch, her body sending
Rayz of lightening from each finger, each
Toe. The blue rayz pointed toward the fourth
Planet south of the glowing axis & its unsuspecting
½ humans ½ beasts who hungered for a full moon
To illuminate the seeds they had just implanted
Into each other.

All that SHE wanted then was to inhabit
The fifth planet of the sky which exploded
Into a billion stars, confetti blessings from
Himself, little fortunes: "you will meet
your future mate on Pluto," "you will have three
sons in rapid succession," "you will have much
Love in your milieu." Fortunes cracked open,
Leaving crumbled cookies behind.

Jimmy whispered her birth name, all vowels:
aayooeeiuuouaa. SHE sang his name shattering
The notes as they broke off into points of light.
He said his name, SHE said hers as they
Orbited the sun, careful not to get burned.
Said their goodbyes.

SHEILA
Sheila has always wanted a Mass
Named after her. A wish upon
A star is but a prayer, oh heavenly
Daddy give me but a little Mass
On which to hang my bonnet,
A Mass rusted with broken pieces
Of mosaics made of all colors
Like a piece of onyx exploded
Into a thousand pieces.

A thousand pieces of Jimmy's body
Is mush, thick as eggnog cut
With E & J VSOP 80 proof,
Turning his flesh a bright copper
Like a young fawn's. "Name a Mass
After me," Sheila says, then Jimmy
Says, "I'll name a planet after you
Once you swim across the galaxy
And return to me in pieces made whole."
But it was the gods who fashioned
The twelfth Mass from the Son, the Holy

Ghost, fourth beneath God and the Holy See.
Sheila says, "so I spread my wings,
Take a deep breath, lift off. I hum
A tune off key, I hum, hmmm,
Hmmmm, hmmmm. That's the correct
Key & I fly across a phalanx of stars:
        Large & small ones,
        Bright & dull ones,
        Near & far ones.
        Pointed ones."
Sheila says, "I come back to Jimmy,
In a thousand pieces made whole."

Sheila is a boat moored to the dock. Washed
Up to the shore. Seaweed lays plastered
On the bow, on the stern like hair trapped
In a bathroom drain, falling out of her head
Because the destruction is eating her up
From inside, cells she cannot see
That can't be trapped or stopped
From multiplying & surging through
Her body like ants at a picnic swarming
The food carrying away 10-50 pounds times
Their body weight.  Sheila watches the ants
Go marching three by three the little one
Skins his knee & they all go
Marching down to the earth to get out
Of the rain boom, boom, boom. The ants
Are sprawling like the mold
On her bathroom shower curtain
& on the wall in her kitchen cabinet
Under the sink drain pipe. Low-income
Housing, no maintenance man or caretaker
On the premises.

SHE
Night sky. Midnight blue. At the
Juke joint on Mars, the saxophonist

Played his last sad note & Jimmy
Dipped her one last time, lifting
Her left thigh with his right hand balancing
The bulk of her body with his left as SHE
Arches backward, small breasts pouting
At the ceiling, woven hair almost sweeping
The floor, the $300 units worth
It for that last minute dip. SHE knew someone
Was taking a picture of them, they
Being the stars of this Martian juke.
The photo would take up much real estate
On the society page of *The Mars Times*.
Why shouldn't it, they were the dull copper
Of imploded skin the color of eggnog,
So cloyingly sweet if not cut with E & J
VSOP 80 proof. Proof that all things that looked
Good didn't necessarily taste good. SHE knew
That Jimmy played around, especially with earth
Wymyn, especially with that one, that Sheila who
He loved as much as he lusted after her.

SHE couldn't see what he saw in Sheila.
Riding in that steel chair, a silver chariot
Streaking across a midnight blue sky.
True, legs weren't a qualification for admittance
Into the juke as there were men missing
One or both legs, women missing one
Or both arms, and there were even a few
Headless Martians who whiled away
An evening or three waiting for that last
Call for alcohol. They'd order three tequila
Shots apiece, knock them back quickly
Then search out who they could find
For that last belly-rubbing, dipping,
Couples Only dance.

Tonite was her time to be swept away
In Jimmy's arms. SHE hadn't seen any

More than five or six earth girls here
This nite & Sheila wasn't one
Of them. Amen & hallelujah
Because SHE couldn't compete with love
This close to Heaven which was all about
Love feeding the Martian multitude
With five loaves of banana bread two
Fried cat fish on Friday nights as Martians
Are so likely to do.

Speaking ill of those who are differently-abled
Is as bad if not worse than chattering on
About the dead who could enact revenge returning
To take up residence in your abode spooking
You into joining their long goodbye. Here
In space a differently-abled humanoid
Could exchange her assumed minuses for
Perceived pluses with the bat of an eyelash.
SHE suspected that is what Sheila had done
To get Jimmy's nose wide-open. But SHE didn't
Care right then because tonite Jimmy dipped
Her for Couples Only. He'd saved the last dance for her.

SHEILA
Planets out of alignment. Sheila hangs
A sharp left in her LaSesa spaceship fresh
Off the factory conveyor belt. The LaSesa
Runs on air and star dust the angels
Have purified so there are no fuel emissions.
The stratosphere, even with the misalignment,
Is fresh, clean, and clear. So Sheila doesn't
Understand why she can't make out whether
It's Pluto the Dog or Jimmy the Cricket
Darting out in front of her. Too late to swerve,
Not knowing whether Pluto or Jimmy will go
Left or right Sheila plows straight ahead
Realizes that it's Jimmy's legs that have
Shattered her gravity shield. Poor Jimmy

Will be in a cast on each leg from his ankle
Bones to his thigh bones. He will learn first-hand
What Sheila has known her entire life of being
In a wheelchair. Better to recuperate.

## Black Mary and G-Man

i.

our church didn't believe in
women having a lot of say about things
Black Mary
her mouth open and a long piece of drool
hanging from her bottom lip
propped
against a tree trunk
fantasizes of going to a private garden
where G-Man would
never find her

ii.

Black Mary
prominent stomach
glossy black and silver hair
slender
thinning eyes
watery now
not a woman's face
once beautiful
not marriage, not love
G-Man didn't suffer
it's all rumor
he wants to frighten her
by inhaling deeply
breathing in ammonia.

iii.

G-Man
Black man driving
sex lips and gentle night
always happy and insatiable
handsome comes off

as endless pleasure desire
have mercy on us.

sunset is the saddest light there is
tantalizingly magical moon quivers &
sizzles as burned lights take over the sky

G-Man flicked on the radio
& between sips of tickle wine, sang
*"baby, baby, where did our love go?"*

every whisper lost love
when only everything is romantic
touched paradise and he lay still in her lap
her passion a sign perfect glow
sparkly into silvery darkness dancing
strong perfume
kiss specks bigger than flying bugs

rhythms think how sad love
is like life in prison
a promise there wasn't a soul
anywhere to help us
hunger through
evening.

iv.

daughter (Zenobia) pauses
son (Xavier) gasps
sometimes lies are preferable
to the truth.

Black Mary's lips lopsided
her favorite place might have been
discussed, page by page.
at dinner she says those memories
metaphors mean almost as much

as a brief moment
filled with boxes of the dead
where the ground is
gray cinder blocks and cement.
there is no roof.

v.

Black Mary embraces the gorgeous lawn that is mostly
dandelions,
Black Mary embraces life, chocolate kisses dazzle.
G-Man celebrates beneath her skirt
he wishes it were up to him
together
candle paradise
perfect pleasure.

G-Man says Black Mary
is a wonderful woman and
a friend.  He lives almost
always happy, he is happy
& sulky between awesome
autumn and summer vacation.

vi.

the bus won't wait.
"okay?"
"okay," she says.
Black Mary might ask for a ride.
she's not too popular. If she is,
I'm in more trouble than I thought,
so says G-Man.

backward places
are likely to burst.
please slow your
tender hand fill

my belly with bliss
let's make love
last long.
she's charmingly eccentric
says her daughter and son
loves our father
more than his art
& we come after art.

my grandmother
says Black Mary
my father's mother
died in a car accident
killed herself from grief
unflinchingly. i want to be
strong like that.
i pretend i am her.

i wish i could sing,
says Black Mary
i'm good at math.
i like the fact i'm good at it.
but sometimes i wish
i could sing.

My father
used to walk
the perimeter
of our property,
says Black Mary
stopped, she says,
nodded at what
he had reaped, proud
then went inside
and set up for the day.

vii.

Black Mary said:
when father was gone, erased
the light changed
when he was gone, erased.
more because i was afraid
i pitched a bitch threatened
to slit my wrists
sliced up my pillow
hid his car keys
pulled hair out of my head
refused to pack when it was time
to leave i just stood there
hoping i'd never move
again.

viii.

kids belong somewhere
i suppose.
our kids didn't belong
anywhere, says G-Man.

ix.

Black Mary and G-Man's daughter (Zenobia) says:
her father hardly speaks; her mother doesn't smile
Black Mary and G-Man's son (Xavier) says:
his father draws; his mother narrates.

Black Mary and G-Man evolve, survive
private parts showing.
no Eve, no Adam
we will never understand
people who don't sigh.

x.

*3,6,9*
*the goose drank wine*
*the monkey chewed tobacco*
*on the street-car line.*
*the line broke*
*the monkey got choked*

*and they all went to heaven*
*in a little rowboat ... clap, clap!*

~

*row, row, row your boat*
*gently down the stream*
*merrily, merrily, merrily, merrily*
*life is but a dream.*

...row, row, row your boat
3,6,9
the goose drank wine ...
...gently down the stream
the monkey chewed tobacco
on the street-car line...
... merrily, merrily, merrily, merrily
the line broke
the monkey got choked ...
... life is but a dream
and they all went to heaven
in a little rowboat ... clap, clap!

the gander drank wine, too, after all
what's good for her ... and all that jazz
even though truth be told
she was ole skool and preferred
Brass Monkey chewed tobacco,
we assume he was a male,

female monkeys are called
female monkeys smoke

Marlboro Menthols in the green box
with the line broken
down the middle
of his throat, he choked
and the goose (Black Mary)
merrily, merrily, and the gander
(G-Man) in his little rowboat
will one day go to heaven
dreaming of life
in a dream
clap … clap!

## Black Mary Confesses at the Church

The letter invited me
i accepted for mixed
& selfish reasons.
i became nervous
Being in the presence of
This supreme gift
From Pastor's grace
Dabbled like a painting
Seeing how combining
All matters of life and death,
Drawn on the cardboard church fans
We waved past dampened brows
Was a revelation.

i was an abstract lady.
All questions
About whats and wherefores
An air of mystery.
"i don't wear my hair permed,
i have plenty of hair,
i wear it inside my head,
relished by white gardenias
& purple violets
usually damp like
low spreading
chokecherries."

But the thought of G-Man's recent
Traitorous actions
Rankled in my mind
Cold and aloof
As i walked along
Very anxious to see
Who he would do next.
They were common names:

Susie was the firmest
Frankie was the funniest
Tammi was the fiercest
Rochelle was the freshest
They clung against each other
Chiseled legs and ankles
Just big enough to cross
Connected by crudeness
In theory, responsible
For their bad behavior.

i forgave & forgave & forgave
& then i didn't care any more
While G-Man caroused with
Prostitutes, pickpockets
Rich women, poor women,
Baker women, thieves,
Doctors and so on,
He knew where the door
Was and how to walk through
It while i answered the letter
In my mind on my way
To Church where women have
No say so, so i didn't say
To Pastor that i would pack
Zenobia and Xavier and go.  i didn't
Have any say so, so i didn't
Say to Pastor that i had thought
Of keeping boiling hot grits
On the stove
For the right occasion.

Pastor began to forgive sins
In times of indulgence and poverty
Dependent on the size of sinners' tithes
As Pastor was informed
Of tithes and offerings.
There were Church records

Of personal lives
Struggles,
Frustrations.
Churches were built
By the architects of delusions
A menagerie of mingled dreams.

Pastor's wife told me how to prepare
For Church dinners:
Sharpen your knife on a whet stone
Swipe it at an angle, one side
First then the other, clean it off
Wipe with oil & then:
Sauteed fruits & green vegetables
Roasted turkey
Pigs bar-be-qued on spits
Friday fresh fried fish

Prayers are everything, but no
Hail Mary's: you can't get
To the Son through
His mother, Praise Jesus.
Say the words and all the rest
Will come true in the best
Way that you could ever hope
And give you silent ways to cope
With all that tramples in your life
Be it husband or be it wife
Or children in their times of strife.

Out in the warmth of a spring
Evening, catching fireflies
In mayonnaise jars with breathing
Holes punched in the top: Zenobia
And Xavier loved catching them
On nights G-Man took his sweet time
Coming home. On nights when
i answered Pastor's letter, written

Only to me, and the mail came
When i was home alone.

## G-Man

I be gwoin to de bar wid dis sweet thang
Still hangin' 'tween my legs, stretchin'

My jeans, getting hard fo' Mary who loves me
But don't like me very much. She don't have to say so

It be in de color of her eyes, dat sometimes she despises
The ground I puts my feets on. Could she have read me

All those years ago 'bout my side-stepping wid dat
Riverview gal? Mr. Gene would'n've neva said a word.

And dat was so long ago. Mary ain't happy, I knows
but I don't knows what to do to make the drool stop leaking

From her bottom lip.
I know she don't like my breaf, she turn

Her head away from me when I so near to her
Dear to her as de music play.

## Zenobia Writes About Her Spiritual Death and Becoming

I am always dying, changing
from None-thing
                 into
                        Some-thing. And back, again. A whisper-
willow   girl
                   toddler   enfant   embryo
Some-thing living while I am always dy-
ing, flushed away in times gone past
               at last, in part my heart
                        beating to no rhythm but not de-
feated marching on like the Christian soldiers
with the cross of Jesus
               off to battle no more
                        willing to succumb to forces
I cannot see but can name with the same
words I use to sing spiritual lullabies
               to babes in carriages walking to
                        sanctuaries.
I am always dying, lying in wait for another day another way
to make myself known to the universe: me: a black girl
               swirling through space and time, never with rhyme
                        or reason other than to season the earth
with my magic(k), here I am, there I go, can you catch
me? before I disappear change from None-thing into Some-thing
               can you see my change from black-to-blue
                        ocean and sky, below and above
I am the source of all wisdom: me: a black girl
twirled past ages of spiritual kingdoms
               I ruled like the wee queen I am
                        always taking a stand for the down-trodden
those less fortunate than rulers of civilizations
where spiritual greed superseded spiritual need
               having was more imperative than knowing,
                        giving of knowledge to those in search
Of alphabets made of Sanskrit and hieroglyphics like ones
Found in hallways of ancient tombs

in Saharan deserts near Piscean waters
like those off the Ivory Coast.
I am always dying, changing None-thing into Some-thing becoming
More ancient than mollusks: shrimp and crab and oysters:
than the fishes created before cattle and oxen
and other huge beasts of the earth roamed
the land, a band of dinosaurs, tyrannosaurus Rex; and tarantulas
slithering on their tiny bellies in the rocky terrain brain dead
from all the stinging they do to unsuspecting
souls who crawl on the earth sharing space
with a race of beings who pray to gods and goddesses along the golden
pathways of euphoria, heavenly bliss, desire and circumspect
errors, mistakes made in the name of peace
let us cease with wars that claim
the land where I live, where I am always
dying, a spiritual death that tears my body
from my soul and leaves me in two
pieces, one of limbs and skin and intestinal
bodies: bones heart lungs; the other vocal-chords
vibrate with songs of the soul
turtle doves in a quiet breeze
coo coo coo coo you are spirit:
spirit and breath, inhale and exhale moves the singular leaf
on the low-riding branch of the sycamore tree, breath
trills trills trills trills the buds have song,
too. Quiet little souls, quiet like sleeping
fireflies, their lights dimmed, shuttered by their flapping
wings, headlamps dimly glowing in the shadows
of the forest, for rest in the afterlife
full of strife, where once again we become
kin in one lifetime when the body and soul are realigned
into moveable, breathable, chantable parts sewn together
by sinews, tendons, veins, capillaries,
cells, synapses, thoughts, dreams in which I
am dying, changing from None-thing into Some-thing
memorable, remember me when this you see
and what a girl I used to be a princess
dimensions wide as a mountain

precious as coal into diamonds, water into wine, lightening
into thunder, sea serpents into mermaids into sirens
                men crash into sea boulders at the sound
                        of my sweet melodies my sweet spiritual
delicacies of deliverance from evil for mine is the kingdom
and the power and the glory forever and ever so
                they say, repeat, often-times young
                        girls hear my calls, call back to me
and still, I am dying, always dying, changing from None-thing
into Some-thing spectacular on the horizon, explosive
                firecrackers spitting out rainbows of green,
                        red, blue, golden, pink, azure, yellow
all the colors of spiritual growth known to woman
every twenty-eight days the color of crimson
                fire the blessings come from higher
                        and higher on a scale of one to ten
a spiritual woman who is always dying,
changing from None-thing into Some-thing.

# Kissing Sistuh

i.

When Sistuh and I were children our mother, Black Mary made us pose for a professional photograph kissing each other. I remember feeling embarrassed about kissing a girl, which of course, Sistuh was, not that I had

anything against girls in particular but kissing them was a task I didn't want to undertake not even for a photograph with the one girl I loved in this world, loved even more than Black Mary. It felt strange calling my

mother Black Mary and my twin sister, Sistuh, when her real name was Zenobia. No one in our family called anyone by their real names, even dad was G-Man. G-Man: a superhero replete with red cape who could

fly throughout the stratosphere where Sistuh's unnamed star floated, encased in a golden ring, captured by Wonder Woman's lasso, an exploding planet like Superman's Kyrpton blown to bits, leaving kryptonite as his

Achille's Heel, as G-Man said, "Brutah, being black and gay and out are the only things that can destroy you." But there were other things that could do that: pretending to be someone G-Man wanted.

II.

When Sistuh and I were children our mother, Black Mary, would take us on excursions as she would call them (even then I knew G-Man didn't know multisyllabic words like excursion, Black Mary was always smarter,

weren't girls always smarter?) and we would spend lots of time at the Adler Planetarium because Sistuh wanted to be an astronomer and G-Man had even bought her a telescope so that she could go out on our balcony and see the Milky Way, its stars, four arms wrapped around its bulge like Black Mary would pull us into her front and wrap her arms around us, protectively. But anyway, Sistuh and I would stare into the

universe and while she would give names to the stars, I would stare at Andromeda and in my mind build a world of only boys, with feathered hats, like Black Mary's, and feathered boas, like Black Mary's, and red

heels and red purses like Black Mary's, and we boys would have fashion shows and I would name us all by our holy names, Red Rover, Red Rover send Cee Cee right over, Red Rover send Beulah Bee right over.

III.

Rover, Red Rover, send them all right over and on and on down through the alphabet until I got to M, and all I could think of then was Black Mary because I would always want her to be on my planet, always want mother

to be with me, wherever I go, whoever I be, I was going to have Andromeda shine like the little light in the shine song, I'm going let my little light shine like I shone when Black Mary greased me down with Vaseline,

my knees and elbows and face just like she did Sistuh, my twin, Zenobia, just like she did before she posed us for that photograph Mr. Sutton took of us holding onto each other like we sometimes did in our room at night

when it thundered outside or thundered in the living room when G-Man came home after drinking too much and Black Mary would scream at him, "you promised, you promised" and when we were little we got it confused thinking G-Man promised to come home smelling like liquor, strong, like Black Mary sometimes smelled after she put on too much perfume on Friday nights going to her ladies club, too much woman scent.

## IV.

G-Man made promises he could not keep as he opened his mouth to swallow whiskey or bourbon, whichever Mr. Gene was drinking, and we knew this because Mr. Gene would come over to our apartment smelling like

G-Man did the night before, smelling like strong liquor and wild women. I preferred it when Mr. Gene came over smelling like a man, wearing men's cologne. I had a crush on Mr. Gene, for the longest I loved him

the only person who knew was Sistuh because I told her about all of my crushes as she told me about hers, like her crush on the brown-skinned girl who lived next door to us. I loved Mr. Gene although he

was an older man, just starting to wrinkle at the corners of his eyes, at the corners of his lips that I wanted to kiss when Sistuh and I went over to his apartment for sleepovers when Black Mary and G-Man went out

until they decided that we were old enough to stay home by ourselves and Sistuh let me wear her clothes as we played house: she was the father and I was the mother. We played like this until our parents returned.

## V.

Planets and stars, I wish my life was as simple as Sistuh's even when she was Zenobia. She loved girls but Black Mary and G-Man said it was just a phase she was going through, like my feelings about boys was just something that would go away when I reached a certain age, maybe ten or twelve, hopefully before either and before I started getting beaten up on the playground for staring at the b-ball players' legs in their shorts, their legs

weren't Vaselined but ashy and dirt streaked, muscles bulging when they went out for a lay-up or even half-squatting at the free throw line dribbling the ball four times before swish, through the hoop: one point!

But it was more than a phase that I was going through, (more like the none-thing into some-thing experience that Sistuh would later explain to me when we were seventeen that she felt like dying to the old and being reborn to the new, that's how I felt too.)

But for now when I took off my pajamas and put on her night gown, felt the soft material slide over my body, the ruffles touching my knees tickling the caps, and Sistuh put on my pajamas and buttoned the shirt we felt alive.

**Glisten On My Star Dust**

1.

Igboo says, "emeralds
are better than diamonds.
They glow softly in the dark.
I love to run them thru my fingers
and let them glisten on my star dust."

2.

Today: I couldn't hear birds singing their regular song.
They hiccupped when I screamed "boo;" they weren't scared,
they caught the giggles and giggles floated out of their mouths
ran back in because they got cold, wanted belly warmth.
Tomorrow is a shining glow comfortable as a melody.

3.

I am anticipating the secret to the
underworld of the other creatures.
The keys are coming in the mail
on the fishing line.  Be careful not to
get caught on the hook.  Just take
the envelope off, revealing the golden
keys on page 3 of the booklet.
When you get to page 53 I'll make
the first 10 pages disappear with my
fleeting thoughts.  POOF! On page 53
I'll reverse the order of the words,
you'll see the beginning of the secret.

4.

And so, it's another day, when we swipe
the hours with a very sharp pencil, quick,
on the paper, swish, swish, collectively
crosshatching the lashes of the clock

movement without touching the page
first, then laying down the hours 12, 6
3, finally 9, 2 & 1 oops, 1 & 2, then 4
and 5, 7 & 8, 10 & 11, 24 hours in a
mile of Sundays, skipping church—*all
hail the power of Jesus' name*—then 20
hours blending bridges between eyes and
noses and none of this makes sense
if you don't have a soft pencil with
dark lead, sharpened and whisked
thru a legend.

5.

I'll go see the intrusion.  Go to the kitchen and
get you some gobbledygook to eat and drink or else
we'll have to order out.  No fingers, nuggets, drummies,
wings with buffalo sauce and bleu cheese dressing
on a wooden platter.  You are hungry for something
that food won't satisfy.  But I'll feed you anyway.

6.

Don't perspire, you'll get all foostie and will have to shower
and get all ashy and we're out of lotion with aloe.  So run thru
the sprinkler with all the other Black kids like you've got the sense
God gave a Billy goat, and I know some brilliant GOATS.

7.

If I whisper blue notes in your ear while you're frying
bacon to sauté with the string beans, garlic, and onion,
will you whistle I Will Always Love You and mean it?

8.

Will you come to me in my daydreams or in my lightening nights?
Either way you'll come when the moon has bedded down

the sun, we'll keep each other company until morn,
when rain greys the skies and moistens the roadways.

9.

398.2 and the gamut from 900 to 999:   fairy tales
and slave narratives: the origins of a people vie for attention
from kings and princesses, the pablum of gullible little ones,
learning to talk, to walk.

10.

Written and spoken words.  Children of ancient storytellers
bloom on narrow branches plucked gingerly by skilled
tongues reciting only on full and quarter moons.

11.

Inversion changes lives forever, wipes pain away along spinal
lines made straight with crooked cricks of bone.  Feeling better
after knocking back a shot of whiskey, single-fisted, like
a gambler with a straight flush, king high.

12.

Green-eyed monsters have red skins, blue hair.  Only
chartreuse images wreck the same damage as cyclones
in a dusty town of prairie shores in the middle of the universe.

13.

Stuck on stupid like frostbite on fingertips alliterative
allegories aligned along ailing agendas.  Nonsensical,
I know, but there it is.

14.

A watched pot never boils until you add salt and vegetable

oil, then the water turns into a rolling boil, a tsunami
in steel.  So the old saying like many others isn't true,
or can be altered like a lie.

15.

Igboo says:  I apologize. If you have trauma,
no matter how big or small, I'm there for you. You don't look
good wearing your problems, an error of judgement that can
be remedied whenever you acquiesce to the goddess.

## Moonlight Brings with It
*Inspired by Ross Gay*

This evening my Creature, my Igboo, turns purple
As we walk through all I have created: the orchids
& grape vines, & cannabis bushes, & roadways &
Highways, & skyscrapers, & aeroplanes, & cameras,
& cast-iron skillets, & cows & horses & goats & other
Four-footed animals & the beautiful girls & women
I created in my Image. Igboo is purple with rage,
With an anger only I can interpret because I, too,
Summon anger & rage. I am purple as *the blood*
*That I shed for the long-limbed girls of my past,*
*As curvaceous as the women of my present,*
*As weary as the girls and women I've absorbed*
*Drink & you are of me*, as thinly purple as the silken
Gown & cape that I wear when walking through
Fields of yellow sunflowers so many sunflowers
It looks like my fields are on fire & this is what I see
& feel as I walk alongside Igboo, their wide, long body,
Transparent as crystal but not as delicate as my anger
Although, as I'd previously told you Igboo reads
My thoughts, translates them into this strange
Language called English that they invented so you
Can understand my purple.

But then, moonlight shines on my naked face, neck, shoulders,
Arms, breasts, stomach, mound, thighs, legs, ankles, feet
& especially my toes, beams of moonlight caressing my
Body washing away the anger caused by the animal I created.
That animal tried to talk three of my girls, not yet women,
Into eating the green crab apple which I strictly forbid
Because they were used in slingshots which were only to be
Aimed at the men of Herst, (who knew who gave birth
To them, were they thought into existence like my girls, my
Women, and if so who would think of such beastly beings?)
But the crab apples, particularly the green ones, green
The color of my cannabis bushes, green as envy, darker green
As jealousy, these are the ones slung toward the male creatures,
Not to be mistaken for my Creature, Igboo the Merciful,

Igboo the Great Translator, Igboo my Partner, Igboo
the Gentler & Kinder & now they are turning transparent
With a soothing silver outline so that they or because of me
Can read the words, phonetically, the English that they alone,
Oh no, there is one girlchild who can read the English words—
How she came from me I don't know, she should be
Igboo's child—and she too is flushed clear baby-blue
Veined skin she can pass the test that the other women
Have designed for *irregular* girlchildren. That's what
the women call them not I who will one day absorb
those women and turn them into benign creatures.
But for now, they, like the moonlight, like Igboo,
provide me company,

With joy with laughter at their own expense they
Make this load I carry bearable joyous even. Even now
I am translucent in the moonlight, Igboo can see straight
Through me as I can see through them, Igboo is non-binary,
& I am asexual, what a duo we make: Me & Igboo. Living
In our garden of Cypress living off the land & the water
Everything I created & Igboo named, or I named them
All & Igboo translated my names into English and whatever,
The words churn in my gut up through my throat out
Of my mouth because the moonlight brings satiation,
Satisfaction, stillness from the envy & jealousy of the purple
Which is silken but not red or blue silk & satin that make up
My gowns for meetings with my mother which also happen
During the time of moonlight. She will be here in 22 minutes
When the moonlight is at its brightest, whitest & I will feel
Loved like the baby sparrow secured in its nest guarded
By its hawk godmother. I will be treasured like a baby
Sparrow, more than a chest of jewels. I will be me, transparent
As Igboo. We will become me.

## Portia co-opts history

Portia, Portia, damn near white, auburn shoulder-length hair,
Portia lost to the rapture of her skin. Portia's arms open
and bleeding 14k gold and sweet oils. Portia gathers her body,
and spreads her legs before us, begging to be kissed, tells us,
I love you, as if it wasn't written across her milky pierced breasts.

Portia, the youngest Portia from a long line of Portias, grabs us
by the wrist, and handcuffs us to this room by the strength
of her voice alone. Portia is a lover, is a slut, is a woman
of valor, is Bathsheba, is Ophelia, is Cleopatra, is Nefertiti,
is Sappho, is known only by her first name, is Maya,
is Myrlie, is Coretta, is Rosa, is a rose of Sharon,
is a lily of the valley, is none of these, was the winner
in the end.

Portia only believed in what she saw and what she saw blinded her,
rendered her mute. She co-opts a history she ain't never had.
But didn't I hear her cries from garbage-strewn
sidewalks, from the bowels of roach-infested tenements
with peeling lead-based paint and urine-drenched hallways,
and blood stains on the dance floor, and didn't I grow up
with those very same icons, didn't I?

As Portia speaks, we women hold hands in prayer, our only thoughts
for a drink of wine. We are Babylonians; we speak in every tongue,
emeralds fall from our eyes. We all sing, waiting to be born
inside our heads.

Drenched in the sound of her voice, the sea crashes when she talks.
Portia drags us kicking and screaming like a scratched record
from the comfort of our self-hatred and low self-esteem. We've learned
to appear strong, to appear hard. We are armed against each other,
separated. Our disfigurement is something only other sistahs

recognize,
pretend we do not see. We pray, look away from those who recognize
us.

Portia's is a soft wash of voices chanting on Gullah Island while she
snaps beans and combs nappy heads and greases ashy knees and elbows
and sings hymns and wails a gut bucket of blues, daring every woman
in the room to feed her brain the food of her own history. We let go
of old traumas and receive the blessings and comforts of letting go.
We swallow her speech, wallow in it, wash our bodies in the blood, eat her.

For the first time I recognize myself in Portia's reflection I see myself,
of Portia I sing. Not placing her above the Creatress, she is twelve steps
beyond the rainbow, she skittles across the grain. And I love myself
because I, too, am Portia, of her flesh, she eats my sins. Amen.

**Davida Kilgore** is the author of a short story collection, *Last Summer* and, as Davida Adedjouma, is the editor of an award-winning book of poetry, *The Palm of My Heart: Poetry by African American Children* written by children ages 5-13 who she taught in afterschool programs in St. Paul and Minneapolis. Her work has been produced by SteppingStone Theatre, read on Broadway at Symphony Space, adapted for film, and published nationally and internationally. Davida's fiction recently appeared in the *Water~Stone Review, midnight & indigo,* and *Fantasy Magazine,* her monologues appeared in *2022 Best Women's Stage Monologues* and *2022 Best Men's Stage Monologues,* and her poetry appeared in *I Am, I Can: Poetry About African American Minnesotans with Different Abilities, the Blue Collar Review,* and the anthology *Let the Black Women Say Ase'.* She has been the recipient of fellowships and grants from the Bush Foundation, the Jerome Foundation, and the Minnesota State Arts Board.

www.ingramcontent.com/pod-product-compliance
Lightning Source LLC
Chambersburg PA
CBHW020223090426
42734CB00008B/1190